WREATHS & GARLANDS
for Embroidery

WREATHS & GARLANDS
for Embroidery

Heather Joynes

Kangaroo Press

My most grateful thanks to:

My husband Jack, for his encouragement and help;
Doris Waltho for typing the manuscript;
DMC for supplying the threads used in this book;
Cotton-On Creations for the silk ribbons.

DMC embroidery threads can be obtained at all good embroidery shops.

Silk ribbons as used in this book can be obtained from Merrigang Cottage, PO Box 205, Beecroft NSW 2119.

© Heather Joynes 1994

First published in 1994 by Kangaroo Press Pty Ltd
3 Whitehall Road Kenthurst NSW 2156 Australia
P.O. Box 6125 Dural Delivery Centre NSW 2158
Typeset by G.T. Setters Pty Limited
Printed in Hong Kong through Colorcraft

ISBN 0 86417 640 6

Contents

Introduction

Wreaths and garlands of flowers have long been an inspiration for the decorative arts, and there is something appealingly festive about them. They make a wonderful theme for embroidery as the permutations are limitless, of both the flowers and the techniques of embroidery.

I have chosen to interpret wreaths and garlands in this book in three techniques—stitchery, ribbon embroidery and wool embroidery. I have included notes on materials and equipment, and general hints on each technique. The designs in each of the three sections could be interchanged, so the reader has plenty of choice. I would like to think that some readers would adapt the designs to their own taste, altering the colours or the flowers or the threads and ribbons.

The ideas in this book are meant to be a starting point—to be built on and developed and enjoyed.

Basic Techniques

Equipment

Needles are very important tools and special needles are used for different techniques. It is important to choose the right needle for the thread and fabric you are working with. The needle should take the thread easily and make an adequate hole in the fabric for the thread to pass through.

Crewel needles are used for embroidery with stranded cotton, perle cotton, silk and viscose threads. Tapestry needles are used for wool embroidery, and chenille needles are used in ribbon embroidery.

A good pair of embroidery scissors is essential, and a larger pair of dressmaking scissors is required for cutting fabric.

Embroidery hoops and frames come in various sizes. A collection of several different sizes and types is an asset.

Good hard pencils, felt pens, a compass, steel ruler, metal T square, a craft knife, rotary cutter and cutting board are other very useful things to own.

Fabric glue, adhesive tape, acid free cardboard and frame kits are necessary for finishing pictures and frames.

Fabrics and threads are available in such variety today that choice is sometimes difficult. Always bear in mind the purpose of the article you intend to embroider when you are making purchases.

A collection of different threads builds up gradually as different projects are worked. It is a good idea to organise threads in colour groups. There are thread winders available, and boxes to keep the threads in, which makes selection easier.

Materials and equipment

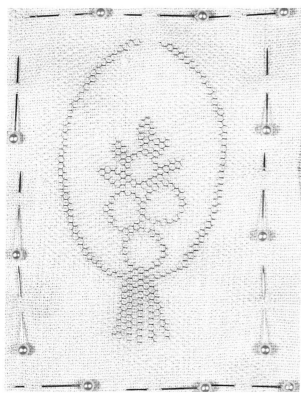
Transferring a design by the net method

Transferring Designs

Only a very simple outline of the design need be transferred to the fabric to be embroidered. Small designs may only need to be indicated by dots for the centres of the flowers and central vein lines for the leaves, while most designs can be followed from a drawing or diagram once the main elements are transferred.

Large or more specific designs can be transferred by tracing onto the material from a drawing with a sharp pencil or water-soluble fabric marking pen, or by the nylon net method. Trace the design onto paper with a black felt pen so that it is very clear. Tape this to a flat surface with adhesive tape. Lay a piece of nylon net over the design, attaching it with adhesive tape. Go over the outline of the design with a black marking pen, then remove the net and place in position on the fabric to be embroidered. Pin or baste securely in place. Now go over the outline on the net with a water-soluble fabric marking pen. When you remove the net, the outline of the design will appear on the fabric as a series of dots. These dots can be removed when the embroidery is finished by holding a cotton bud, dampened with water, against them.

Transferring a design onto dark material presents a more difficult problem. Trace through the net with a dressmaker's chalk pencil. This does tend to rub off while you are working, but the parts not being worked on can be covered with tissue paper pinned to the fabric.

I prefer to mark as little as possible on the fabric, and for dark fabrics to evolve a design that can be worked freehand. This comes with practice.

Designing

The design must be suitable in scale for the article to be made. Always establish the size and shape of the article first, then the area to be embroidered, then the details of the design.

Designing for clothing needs special attention, as the whole garment must be considered as well as the person who will wear it. Cut an extra paper pattern and mark on it the area to be embroidered, then try it against the person who will wear it. Any adjustments can thus be made before working up the design. Time spent planning the design is time well spent and will probably save hours of anguished unpicking.

Try to have a spare piece of the fabric to try out ideas for the embroidery.

Finishing

Finished embroidery can be pressed on the wrong side into a well padded surface—a folded towel is ideal. If any marks remain from an embroidery hoop try spraying them with a fine mist of water and then pressing. Embroidery hoops are not recommended for velvet or velveteen as the marks will not come out. Always take the embroidery out of the hoop when not working on it.

When mounting pictures, make sure the mount is perfectly squared at the corners, and always use acid free board.

If you are working with glue, work over clean white scrap paper and change the paper at every stage of construction. If you get a spot of glue on the embroidery or anywhere else it is not wanted, try removing it with a cotton bud dampened with cheap nail varnish remover—the non-oily sort. This usually works, if you get at it as soon as the damage has been done.

A large darning needle is ideal for spreading glue and for applying a small spot of glue to a small area.

9

STITCHERY

Stitchery is what most people think of as embroidery—stitches with threads. It is usually called surface stitchery in embroidery circles, but because so many embroidery techniques are on the surface this is not really a specific title.

The stitches in this section are all simple and appear, with variations, throughout the book.

The threads and ribbons are readily available from most embroidery shops.

General Hints

Start a stitch with a few small running stitches or a back stitch and then work over them.

To finish a thread, weave it through the back of the stitches already worked.

Always finish a thread at the end of part of the stitch and bring out the new thread where the stitch would continue.

Stitches

Back Stitch

A very simple stitch, giving the effect of a broken line. Useful for outlines, as in the violet leaves on page 39.

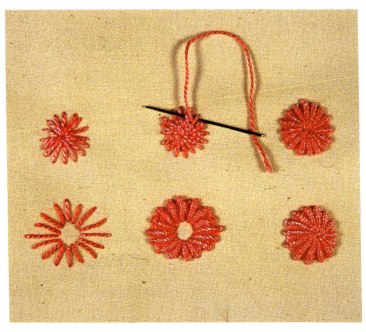

Back-stitched Spider's Web

This stitch starts with a groundwork of spokes in a circle. Sixteen is a good number. Work N, S, E and W first, then fill in three more in each space. Bring the thread up in the centre and take the needle back over a spoke then under the next one. Continue until the circle is filled in.

Ovals can also be worked this way—just make the spokes a little longer in the centre of opposite sides.

Also shown is a circle worked off centre. Both the oval and off-centred web have to be finished by working on a few spokes at the sides instead of going all round the circle.

A space can be left in the centre for groups of knots. This makes a nice flower. See the wreath on page 15.

Buttonhole Stitch

Buttonholing makes good flowers when worked in a circle. This stitch has been used on the wreath on page 15, the jumper on page 62 and the bag on page 58.

Couching

Good for creating a smooth outline, and can be seen in the Wildflower Wreath on page 23, where it is worked as grevillea leaves.

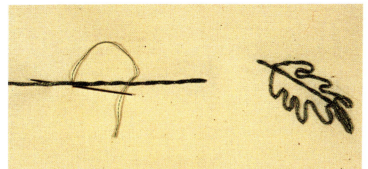

Detached Chain

A most useful stitch. It can be used as a filling stitch, as on the banksia in the Wildflower Wreath; grouped to form leaves, or lavender flowers (see page 19). Worked in a circle it can form flowers, as on the bag on page 58.

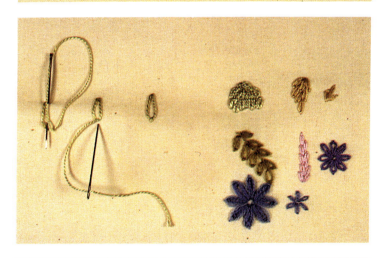

Fly Stitch

Fly stitch can be varied in many ways. It can form flowers or leaves, as on the bag on page 58, or feathery foliage and bottlebrush flowers—see the wreath on page 23.

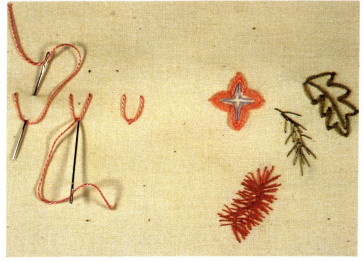

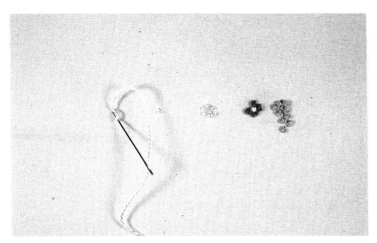

French Knot

The secret of a good French knot is to wind the thread around the needle once only. If a bigger knot is required use double thread or thicker thread. As well as flower centres groups of French knots can be used to make racemes of flowers, like the ones on the frame on page 35.

Oyster Chain Stitch

This stitch needs a little practice to be able to remember it. Start with a twisted chain, then pass the needle and thread underneath the stitch at the top (not through the fabric). Do not pull tight, as this will distort the stitch. Then bring the thread around the stitch and put the needle in the loop at the side and bring out directly under the stitch.

This stitch can be worked continuously in a line, or as single stitches. In a circle it makes a flower, as on the jumper on page 62.

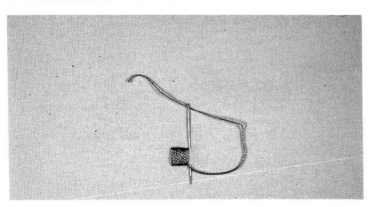

Satin Stitch

Really, satin stitch is straight stitches worked close together. It is best worked with a single thread, otherwise it is difficult to get it to lie smooth. It is worked as a bow on the Lavender Wreath on page 19.

Stem Stitch

Stem stitch makes a very good line and can be used for outlines and stems, and also as a filling stitch. Working the stitch with the thread above the needle gives a smoother line.

Straight Stitch

Straight stitch makes round flowers if worked in a circle. Work N, S, E and W first, then fill in. Flowers in straight stitch appear on many designs in this book.

A rose in straight stitch appears here and in the wreath on page 15.

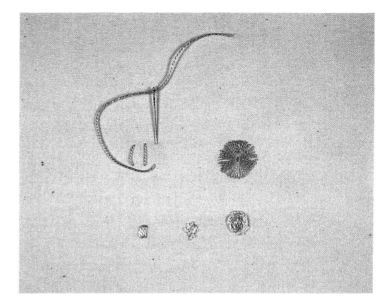

Twisted Chain

A chain stitch with a little difference. It can be worked in a line or a circle or can be used to make sprays of flowers, as on the wreath on page 58.

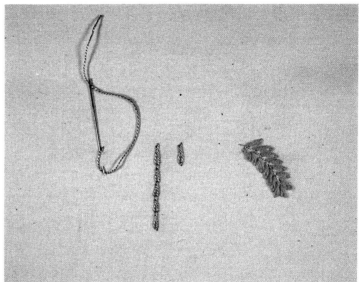

Floral Wreath

This pretty floral wreath, here worked as a picture, could also be worked on a bag or box top.

You will need:
red hoop frame 18 cm (7⅛'') diameter
circle of cardboard 18 cm (7⅛'') diameter
piece of dark blue fabric 24 cm (9½'') square
    (the framed picture is worked on polyester, but cotton, linen, velveteen or rayon would also be suitable)

DMC Stranded Cotton in:
    variegated red
    mauve 211
    yellow 725
    white
DMC Perle No. 5 in:
    variegated pink 48
    red 600
viscose stranded thread in variegated green
fabric glue
crewel needles Nos 9 and 6

Detail of stitchery

Opposite: Floral Wreath worked on polyester

14

 Back-stitched spider's web

Buttonhole stitch

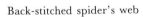 Straight stitch with fly stitch edge

 Straight stitch rose

Fly stitches

 French knots

 Detached chain stitch

Flowers and Bows

Loop Flowers

Five or six loops of ribbon worked in a circle make a lovely flower. The underneath of the tip of the loop needs to be stitched to prevent the loop pulling out. Leave the loop a little loose, do not pull it too tight when sewing down.

Clusters of small loops make very pretty flower heads. Bring the loops through the fabric close together, then work a French knot in the centre of each loop, as the flower at top right in the flower sampler on page 34.

Spider's Web

This is one of the most useful stitches for ribbon embroidery, as it makes very good roses. Work a groundwork of five spokes in a circle—a fly stitch with a stitch on either side is the easiest way to do this. Bring the ribbon out at the centre of the web and weave over and under the spokes, round and round until the web is filled. Do not pull the ribbon tight while weaving—leave it just a little loose, and let it twist now and again, as this adds to the natural look of the rose. Try using two or three shades of ribbon around the web.

Carnations

To make a small carnation take 20 cm (8'') of 4 mm (⅛'') silk ribbon, fold it in half and whip over one side of the doubled ribbon with fine thread. Gather up carefully to about 4 cm (1½''). Pin in place and sew down as invisibly as possible. This is fiddly, as the gathered ribbon tends to twist. Sew one end to the centre of the flower, then pin around in a small circle. Tuck the other end under the frill and finish off.

Petal Stitch

This is easiest worked with 7 mm (¼'') silk ribbon. Bring the ribbon through the fabric at the centre of the flowers. Hold flat while putting the needle through the ribbon at the end of the petal. Pull through to the back of the fabric gently, leaving a curl at the end of the petal.

Rosebuds

Thread two shades of 4 mm (⅛'') silk ribbon into one needle, a chenille needle for preference. Bring through the fabric and make two straight stitches, one almost on top of the other. In thread add a fly stitch around the bud and a straight stitch from the centre of the fly stitch.

Bows

Tie a ribbon bow and sew the knot at the centre in place in the design. Then pin the bow out to the required shape and sew down the edges of the ribbon with tiny stitches and fine thread, using a fine needle. If using bows on clothing, as on the jumper on page 43, stem stitch can be worked on the edges of the ribbon. This gives a very good finish and attaches the ribbon firmly to the garment.

To make a bow with three loops tie a bow loosely then thread one end of the ribbon through the knot at the centre. Pull the first loops of the bow tightly, then stitch at the knot to secure. The stitches need to be tiny and as invisible as possible. Stitch in place at the knot, then pin out the bow and stitch on the edges of the ribbon with tiny stitches and matching thread. Make sure the needle is not piercing a ribbon already worked, as this can have disastrous results!

(Flowers and bows are illustrated on the following page.)

Ribbon flower sampler shows:
top row—loop flowers
middle row—spider's web rose, rosebuds
bottom row—carnation, petal stitch

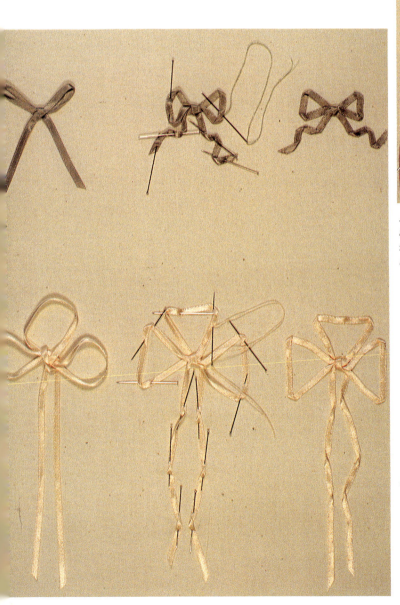

Ribbon bows

Opposite: Wreathed Frame worked on moiré (page 36)

34

Wreathed Frame *Illustrated on previous page*

You will need
fabric approximately 30 cm × 25 cm (12″ × 10″)
cardboard frame kit approximately 24.5 cm ×
    19.5 cm (9½″ × 7½″)
50 cm (½ yd) 4 mm (⅛″) apricot satin ribbon
3.5 m (3½ yds) 7 mm (¼″) silk ribbons in:
    apricot 39
    yellow 172
    white
3.5 m (3½ yds) 7 mm (¼″) organdie ribbons in:
    tan 67
    yellow 8
3.5 m (3½ yds) 4 mm (⅛″) silk ribbons in:
    pinks 103, 104
    yellows 13, 14
DMC Perle Cotton No. 8 in:
    gold 977
    ecru
DMC Stranded Cotton in:
    variegated green 92
    green 3013
    mauve 3743
chenille and tapestry needles No. 20
crewel needles Nos 6 and 9
fabric glue

Transfer the design to the fabric by the net method described on page 9. Transfer as little as possible—just dots for the centres of the flowers and the centre lines for the sprays of leaves. It is quite possible to work from the drawing once the main elements of the design are established.

Start with the bow. Take 35 cm (14″) of the satin ribbon and tie in a bow, pin out and stitch in place (see page 34).

Work the large flowers next, using the 7 mm (½″) apricot and yellow silk ribbons, and the tan and yellow organdie ribbons. Take 30 cm (12″) of the apricot silk ribbon and the tan organdie ribbon; thread both in the same chenille needle and work six petals in petal stitch. This is most easily done if two petals are worked opposite each other first, then two, evenly spaced, each side of these. Work one flower in apricot silk and yellow organdie ribbons. Centres of the flowers are six French knots in gold Perle No. 8.

Work the small spray of leaves, rosebud and mauve flowers in the bow next. The leaves are in detached chains with a straight stitch within them, on a stem of stem stitch, using three strands of the variegated green cotton.

The rosebuds are made with two lengths of pink ribbons 103 and 104 in the same needle. Make two straight stitches the length of the bud, one stitch almost on top of the other. Let the ribbon twist a little so that both colours show. Work a fly stitch around the bud and a straight stitch from the centre of it into the bud. The mauve spray is French knots in six strands of mauve 3743.

The white flowerhead is in loops of 7 mm (¼″) white ribbon (see page 37), each loop held down at the centre with a French knot in four strands of variegated green thread.

Work the three spider's web roses next, two in pink 104 and one in 103, varying the size a little. The leaves, rosebuds and mauve sprays follow, worked as before.

The green spray has three large fly stitches, of uneven length and worked one inside the other, in two strands of green 3013. French knots in four strands of the same green and some in the variegated thread are worked at the ends of the fly stitches.

The yellow roses are worked in spider's web stitch, one in each yellow.

There are small groups of five French knots worked in ecru Perle No. 5 here and there among the flowers.

Follow the design around the frame.

When finished, press lightly on the wrong side into a well padded surface.

To make up
Trim the fabric to about 2 cm (¾″) of the cardboard frame. Pin the embroidered fabric to the

Petal stitch

Loop flowers

Straight stitches

Spider's web

Stem stitch stem
Detached chain leaves

French knots

Fly stitch

Detail of ribbon embroidery

outer edge of the frame, sticking the pins into the edge of the cardboard. Work on opposite sides, pinning from the centres out. Make sure the embroidery is centred and in the right place.

Lay the frame face down onto a clean surface (an old sheet or towel is ideal). Run a gathering thread around the rounded corners and pull it up until it fits snugly.

Using a good fabric glue, glue the fabric around the edge of the frame, working on one side at a time, then the opposite side. Pull the fabric so that it is taut. Leave till the glue is dry—this should take only about 5–10 minutes.

Next cut out the oval in the centre of the frame leaving 2 cm (¾'') turning all round. Do this from the back as this way you can see what you are doing. Make cuts to within a millimetre of the frame, all around the oval.

Put the frame face down again on the clean surface and then put glue around the edge of the oval on the cardboard. Turn the cut edges of the fabric over onto the glue, pulling firmly. You should have a clean line around the frame, with no gathers or puckers.

Centre the picture or photograph you are framing and tape the corners to the frame with sticky tape. Put glue around the edge of the back of the frame and glue it to the backing piece.

If the picture is to be hung glue a small curtain ring with ribbon threaded through it to the back of the finished frame.

A stand can be made from a piece of card approximately 5 cm (2'') wide scored across 4 cm (1½'') from one end to form a hinge. Adjust the length to the length of the frame so that it stands almost upright.

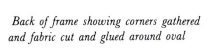

*Back of frame showing corners gathered
and fabric cut and glued around oval*

Violet Garland worked on a pure cotton T shirt (page 40) with detail of ribbon embroidery below

Violet Garland *Illustrated on previous page*

The T shirt illustrated is pure cotton and was easy to work on with 4 mm (⅛'') silk ribbons. Polyester satin ribbons would not be suitable, as they are hard to pull through on fine knit fabric. Blouses or tops in other fabrics such as linen, cotton or rayon would also be suitable for this design.

You will need
T shirt or top
8 m (8 yds) 4 mm (⅛'') white silk ribbon
DMC Stranded Cotton in:
    violet 552
    white
chenille needle No. 18
crewel needle No. 9

It should not be necessary to transfer the design onto the fabric as it is quite easy to freehand it from the diagram. Not every flower and leaf is the same, which adds to the charm of the design.

Start at the centre back, as any discrepancies there will not be as obvious as on the front. When you feel completely confident, start at the centre front and work towards each shoulder.

The violets have five petals, each one of two straight stitches almost on top of one another, worked in the white silk ribbon. There are two petals fairly close at the top, one at each side, and a wide one below—this one actually has three stitches in it.

The violet centres are worked in one strand of violet 552, also in straight stitches, uneven in length.

Buds are two straight stitches with stem stitch stems in one strand of white cotton. A small fly stitch is worked around the bud in white.

Leaves are in back stitch using two strands of white cotton.

jo

Continue around the back of the garment in the same manner

To prevent rubbing or wear on the back of the embroidery add a strip of iron-on interfacing over it, cut to the shape of the neckline. Make sure that all ends of ribbon are securely sewn down.

Embroidery with silk and polyester ribbons can be washed with care. Hand washing is best, and spin drying is recommended. Colours are fast and I find that clothing embroidered with ribbons washes very well—with care.

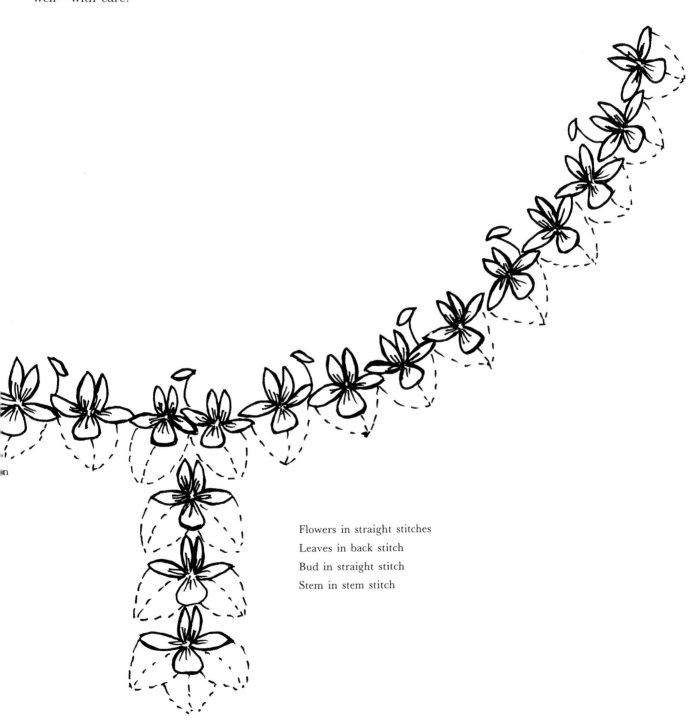

Flowers in straight stitches
Leaves in back stitch
Bud in straight stitch
Stem in stem stitch

Blue Garland

This design, suitable for a jumper or top, is shown worked on a commercially made jumper. Close knit cotton or polyester fabrics are not easy to work on whereas the average hand or machine knitted garment is ideal.

You will need
jumper or top with V neck
2.5 m (2½ yds) 7 mm (¼'') double-sided satin ribbon in slate blue

3 m (3 yds) 7 mm (¼'') nylon ribbon in sky blue
3 m (3 yds) 7 mm (¼'') silk ribbon in pale blue
3 m (3 yds) 4 mm (⅛'') double-sided satin ribbon in soft blue
3 m (3 yds) 4 mm (⅛'') silk ribbon in pale blue
DMC Perle No. 5 in dark blue 791
lime green velvet yarn *OR*
    lime green 4 mm (⅛'') satin ribbon
fine sewing cotton to match the slate blue ribbon and the nylon and silk ribbons
chenille needle No. 20

Blue Garland worked on a cream knitted jumper

Opposite: Detail of ribbon embroidery

Start by sewing the wavy line around the V neck, using the slate blue ribbon. Pin the ribbon first, then sew with very small stitches along the edges of the ribbon, working from side to side.

Next, tie three bows in the same ribbon, using 50 cm (½ yd) for each bow. Pin these out and stitch them at the centre of the V and at each shoulder. See page 33 for instructions for pinning out bows.

The large flowers are worked next. Make six loops in a circle, fastened down with a stitch in the end of each loop, for the larger size, and five loops in a circle for the slightly smaller ones. Use the 7 mm (¼'') nylon ribbon for the six-loop flowers and the silk ribbon for the five-looped ones. The centres are worked in French knots in velvet yarn.

Groups of three detached chains are worked alternately in the 4 mm (⅛'') satin ribbon and the 4 mm (⅛'') blue silk ribbon.

The French knots in dark blue Perle No. 5 are worked with double thread.

Make sure that all ends of ribbon and threads are securely sewn down at the back.

To prevent the ribbons and threads being rubbed or worn at the back sew a bias strip of silk or polyester over the back of the embroidery, taking care that the stitching does not show on the front.

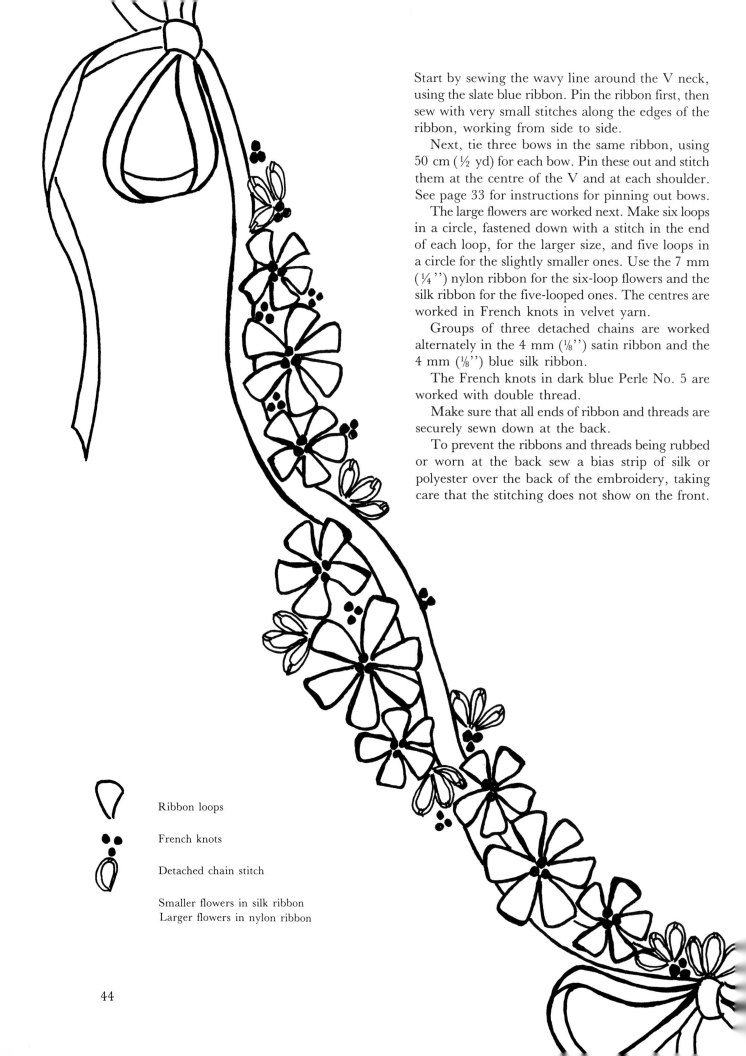

Ribbon loops

French knots

Detached chain stitch

Smaller flowers in silk ribbon
Larger flowers in nylon ribbon

44

Small Wreaths and Garlands

These designs are suitable for a range of items. Lingerie bags, sachets, cards, boxes, clothing and work bags are just some of the things that could be worked.

The fabric in the illustration is calico, but any firm fabric would be suitable.

Small Wreath

You will need
1 m (1 yd) 4 mm (⅛'') silk ribbon in:
    pink 163
    fawn 105
    brown 139
DMC Stranded Cotton in:
    mauve 3041
    green 472
25 cm (10'') firm 2 mm (¹⁄₁₆'') double-sided satin
    ribbon
chenille needle No. 18
crewel needle No. 9
fabric suitable for the project

Draw a 6 cm (2⅜'') diameter circle on the fabric with a sharp pencil, or baste a circle on the fabric. This is easiest done with a circle cut out of firm paper, pinned to the fabric and drawn or basted around.

First tie a bow, pin out and sew down as shown on page 33. Start the flowers at the top of the wreath.

The larger flowers are made with straight stitches, having the ribbon double in the needle, with five petals to each flower. The centre is a French knot in six strands of mauve 3041.

The groups of three small flowers are loops in fawn 105 with a French knot at the centre of each loop in three strands of green 472.

The buds are in brown 139, using two straight stitches for each bud.

French knots in six strands of mauve cotton are worked amongst the flowers, and feathery foliage in fly stitches in one strand of green cotton completes the design.

Mauve Wreath

You will need
fabric for the project
1 m (1 yd) 4 mm (⅛'') green double-sided satin
    ribbon
3 m (3 yds) each of 4 mm (⅛'') silk ribbons in
    mauves 83, 100, 178
DMC Stranded Cotton in yellow 441
fine sewing cotton to match the green ribbon
chenille needle No. 18
crewel needle No. 9

Draw or baste a 10 cm (4'') diameter circle on the fabric, using the method above. Pin, then sew, a wavy line over this circle in the green satin ribbon. With 20 cm (8'') of green ribbon, tie a bow, pin out and sew in place at the centre top of the circle, a little below the wavy line.

Mark the curved lines of the design either with a pencil or basting. This is best done after the green ribbon has been sewn on.

The sprays of flowers are worked with loops of ribbon with a French knot at the centre of each loop worked in two strands of the yellow cotton. Use the three shades of mauve with the deepest colour at the base of each spray and the palest one at the tip.

Oval Wreath

You will need
fabric for the project
1 m (1 yd) 4 mm (⅛'') silk ribbon in:
    old rose 159
    pale rose 163
    dark red 114

45

Small wreaths and garlands worked on calico

    Straight stitches

 Spider's web

 Gathered flower (carnation)

 French knots

  Loop flowers

 Stem stitch

 Detached chains

 Fly stitches

greens 20 and 71
25 cm (10'') green double-sided satin ribbon
DMC Stranded Cotton in green 472
tapestry and chenille needles No. 18
crewel needle No. 9

Draw or baste the oval onto the fabric. (See instructions for the small wreath.) Work over this line in stem stitch with two strands of green 472. Add seven or eight stems at the bottom in stem stitch.

Work the roses in spider's webs, making the centres in the dark red ribbon. The lowest rose is finished in old rose, the two side by side have all three colours and the top one is completed with the pale rose. Buds are worked with the two rose tones threaded into one needle, using a straight stitch. A fly stitch in two strands of green cotton is worked around each bud with a straight stitch added from the centre.

Stems are in stem stitch with two strands.

The leaves around the oval are worked in straight stitches, mostly in the darker green with an occasional lighter green leaf.

Tie a bow in the satin ribbon and pin out then sew down.

Garlands

You will need
fabric for the project
50 cm (½ yd) 4 mm (⅛'') double-sided satin
    ribbon in soft green
2 m (2 yds) each 4 mm (⅛'') silk ribbons in:
    rose 163
    pink 144
    mauve 83
DMC Stranded Cotton in:
    mauve 3743
    yellow 745
    green 3364
Chenille needle No. 18
Crewel needle No. 9

Draw or baste the lines of the two garlands onto the fabric. If possible trace them from the book, otherwise cut paper to the shapes and draw or baste around it.

Start at the centre of the top garland and work the carnations first. These are in the rose silk ribbon, gathering up an 8 cm (3'') length of double ribbon (see page 33).

The little flowers comprise four small straight stitches in the pink and mauve ribbons, with a French knot at the centre in two strands of yellow 745. Vary the two colours, with a few more flowers in one tone.

The groups of leaves are in detached chain stitches with one strand of green cotton.

When both garlands are completed, cut the green ribbon in half and tie two bows. Pin them out and sew down.

One garland only may be sufficient for some items. This type of design can be varied in colour and in flowers used.

WOOL EMBROIDERY

Embroidery with wool has a heavier texture than embroidery in other threads. The wool threads can vary in weight from a thick tapestry wool to a fine crewel wool. Knitting wool can also be made use of, and the addition of other threads can give you contrasts of texture.

No special equipment is needed other than a selection of tapestry needles. Sizes 18–22 are most useful.

To thread wool into a needle, double the wool over the needle and hold it firmly between thumb and forefinger, pull the wool off the needle and thread the small loop through the eye.

To start with tapestry wool, leave an end long enough to thread at the back of the work; when a few stitches have been worked thread the end through the back of the stitches. Finish in the same way.

Thinner crewel wools can be started with a few running stitches or a back stitch and worked over.

Bullion Knots and Roses

Take a stitch the length required for the knot, taking the needle through to the eye. Wind the thread clockwise around the needle as many times as it will take to fill the length of the stitch. Hold the twists firmly with one hand and pull the needle and thread through with the other. Pull up tightly, adjusting the twists if necessary. They should be tight and even. Put the needle through the fabric at the end of the first stitch. If there is a space at this end, there are not enough twists. It takes a little practice to achieve a really good bullion knot.

Bullion roses start with either a tightly packed group of French knots in ecru perle cotton No. 5 or three bullion knots in the same thread. Around the centre work three or four bullion knots with nine twists in ecru tapestry wool, overlapping them. Continue in the same way, increasing the twists around the needle to ten for one row, then twelve and fourteen for the other rows. Change to white tapestry wool for the last row. Use a large darning needle.

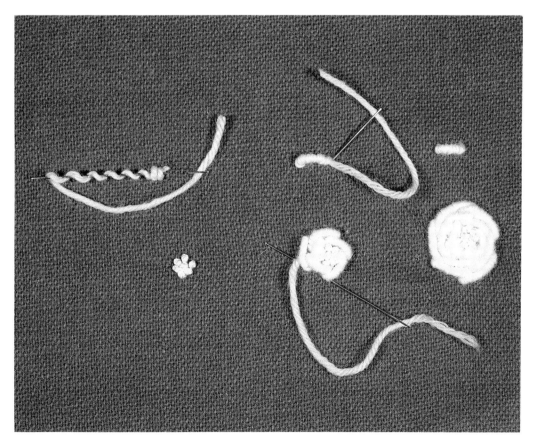

Bullion knots and roses

White Roses

This very pretty cushion is worked on a wool fabric with a firm, but not tight, weave. Other fabrics can be used but they must not be tightly woven, otherwise it will be difficult to pull the tapestry wool through. The Turkish corners on the cushion are a little different and make a nice finish.

This project combines wool embroidery with stitchery and ribbon embroidery.

You will need

wool fabric 84 cm × 50 cm (33'' × 20'')
3 m (3 yds) 4 mm (⅛'') double-sided satin
  ribbon in cream
3 m (3 yds) 15 mm (½'') rayon ribbon in cream
DMC Tapestry Wool in white and ecru
  (2 skeins each)
DMC Perle No. 5 in ecru

Detail of wool embroidery

Opposite: White Roses cushion—wool embroidery on wool

Bullion knots

Loop flowers

Fly stitches

French knots

DMC Stranded Cotton in ecru, white and
  yellow 745
large darning needle
chenille needle No. 20
straw needle No. 5
crewel needles Nos 6 and 9
30 cm (12'') zip
sewing cotton to match fabric
38 cm (15'') square cushion pad

Cut a piece of the fabric 40 cm (16'') square.

Cut out a 21 cm (8½'') diameter circle in paper.
Pin in place in the centre of the fabric and baste
around it. Remove the paper.

Mark dots for the centres of the roses with a
water-soluble fabric marking pen or a couple of
stitches. The design can then be worked freehand
from the diagram.

Start the roses with either three bullion knots for
the profile flowers or seven French knots for the full-
face flowers in the ecru Perle No. 5. Use the straw
needle. With ecru tapestry wool and the large
darning needle make three bullion knots with nine
twists around the needle around the Perle knots.
Work two or three more with ten twists around the
needle, then change to white wool and finish with
knots with twelve twists, then fourteen twists, around
the needle.

Buds are made with two bullion knots in the Perle
No. 5 and two in wool. A fly stitch in six strands
of the yellow stranded cotton is worked around each
bud.

The white sprays beside the roses have stems of
three fly stitches of uneven length, worked one inside
the other with three strands of ecru stranded cotton.
The French knots are in six strands of white cotton.

The sprays of ribbon flowers in cream rayon
ribbon are worked in loops with a French knot in
six strands of yellow stranded cotton at the centre
of each loop. See page 33 for details of loop flowers.

To make each bow take 50 cm (½ yd) of the
cream satin ribbon and tie a loose bow then thread
one end of the ribbon through the centre of the knot
to form a third loop. Pin out in place, then stitch
with tiny stitches along the edges with matching
cotton. See page 34 for details.

To make up
Cut the remaining fabric in half, then trim to two
pieces 40 cm × 22 cm (16'' × 9''). Join the two
pieces for 6 cm (2½'') at each end of one 16 cm
side. Sew the zip in the space between. Open the
zip. With right sides together, join the embroidered
fabric to the piece with the zip.

To make the Turkish corners, measure 4 cm
(1½'') from the tip of each corner along the seams
and mark with a pin. Put one hand into the corner
and with the other hand sew a running stitch in a
circle around the corner from the pins, over the
opened out seams. Pull up and twist the thread
tightly around the stitching several times and fasten
off securely. See the photograph. Do *not* trim as the
surplus in the corners fills them out. Turn right side
out and press carefully. The cushion pad should be
a fraction larger than the cover to fill the cushion
out well.

Steps in making a Turkish corner on a cushion

Garland for Blue Daisies

This design is shown as a tea cosy, but could easily be adapted for a tablecloth or other items of table linen.

You will need
white linen or linen/polyester 38 cm × 60 cm (15'' × 24'')
DMC Medici Wool in blues 8270, 8333, 8899
DMC Perle No. 5 in yellow 307
1 m (1 yd) of double-sided blue satin ribbon 10 mm wide (⅜'')
tapestry needle No. 20
crewel needle No. 6

Cut the linen in half lengthwise to give two pieces 38 cm × 30 cm (15'' × 12'').

Transfer the design to the fabric, either by placing it over the diagram in the book and tracing with a sharp pencil or water-soluble marking pen, or by the net method described on page 9. Mark only the centres of the flowers and the stem lines.

Start at the centre of the design with the large full-face daisies which are worked in blue 8270 using two threads. Each flower has eight petals worked in detached chains with a straight stitch within each one. Work N, S, E and W first, then fill in one stitch between each pair.

The centres are in yellow Perle No. 5, using double thread and making six French knots in each centre.

The large profile daisies are worked in a similar manner using blue 8333 and two threads.

The small daisies are in blue 8899 using one thread only, six detached chains to each flower.

Detail of wool embroidery

54

Stems are worked in stem stitch in one thread of blue 8270.

To make up
Press the embroidery carefully on the wrong side on a well padded surface.

Place the two pieces of linen together, right sides facing; pin around the two sides and across top. Sew up. A 2 cm (¾'') seam is allowed. Trim seam and zigzag.

Press a 3 cm (1¼'') hem with 1 cm (⅜'') turn-under on the lower edge. Hem by hand.

Cut the ribbon in half and tie two bows, then stitch them to the ends of the garlands.

A separate padded lining is made in white cotton and polyester batting.

Garland of Blue Daisies on a tea cosy

join

 Detached chain stitches
and straight stitch within

French knots

Fly stitches

Stem stitch

56

join

Floral Wreath

This brightly coloured wreath looks best on a dark colour and is shown here on black cotton twill. It is embroidered in DMC Medici Wool and some DMC Flower Thread. Both are fine threads and beautiful to sew with.

You will need
50 cm (½ yd) of 115 cm (45'') black twill
DMC Medici Wools in:
   red 8666
   oranges 8908, 8940, 8128
   pink 8133
   yellows 8026, 8748
   greens 8402, 8419
   mauve 8397
   white
   blue 8800
DMC Flower Thread in blues 2358, 2359
crewel needles Nos 5 and 6
50 cm (½ yd) iron-on interfacing
50 cm (½ yd) lining
black sewing cotton

Floral Wreath worked on black cotton twill handbag

two 30 cm (12'') lengths of 1 cm (⅜'') diameter
   dowel
four screw eyes
ball of black knitting wool for a twisted cord
2 m (2 yds) nylon blind cord for piping

Cut a piece of fabric 40 cm × 32 cm (16'' × 12½''). The design is repeated four times around a 16 cm (6½'') diameter circle. To ensure that the completed circle is true it is advisable to baste three concentric circles onto the fabric. This is easiest done by cutting three circles in paper, 10 cm (4''), 16 cm (6½'') and 21.5 cm (8½''). Pin the 16 cm (6½'') circle in place on the fabric, centred 8 cm (3⅛'') from one edge. Baste around the edge of the paper. Repeat with the other two circles.

Fold the 16 cm paper circle in four, open out and place on the fabric again and mark the quarters of the circle with a pin or two or three stitches.

Rather than transfer the design to the fabric, which is more difficult on a dark fabric, draw in the lines of the leaf sprays and circles of flowers with a dressmaker's chalk pencil. Work on one quarter of the design at a time. The design may vary slightly, but will not be obvious.

Start the embroidery with one of the large red flowers on the quarter points. The flower is worked in detached chain stitches using two threads of orange 8128 with another chain inside it in red 8666, also in two threads. The flower has twelve petals and is oval, so make the petals at the sides a little longer. Work N, S, E and W first, then fill in two petals between each pair. Four French knots form the centres, in two threads of yellow 8026.

The saw-toothed leaves are in green 8402 and 8419. Work the central vein first in one thread of 8402, and the outline in two threads in fly stitches.

Detail of wool embroidery

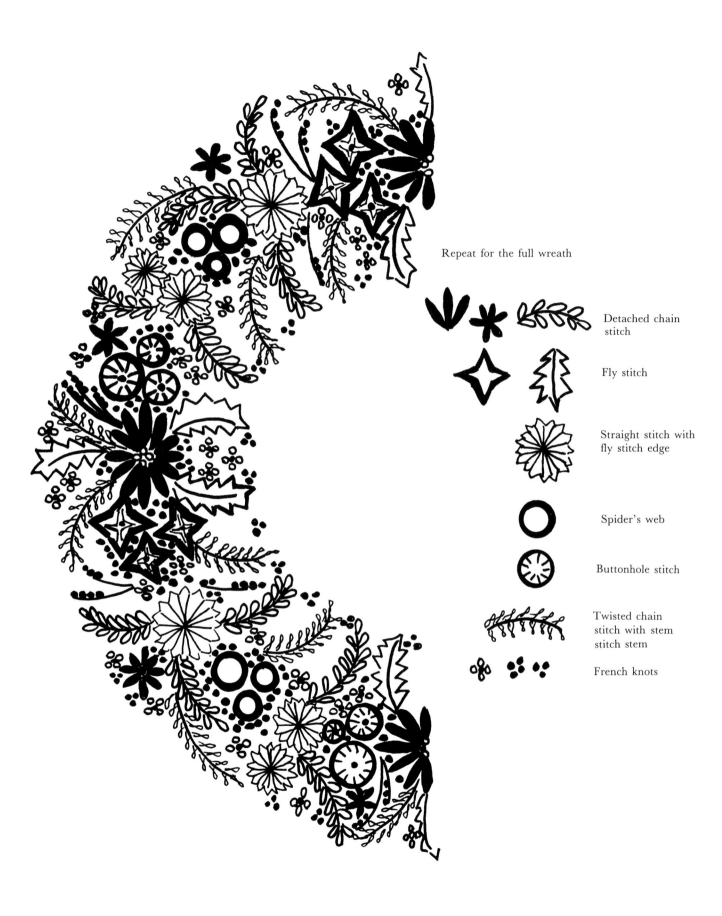

Repeat for the full wreath

Detached chain
stitch

Fly stitch

Straight stitch with
fly stitch edge

Spider's web

Buttonhole stitch

Twisted chain
stitch with stem
stitch stem

French knots

Another row of fly stitches in two threads of 8419 completes the leaf.

Work the star-shaped pink and blue flowers next. These have four petals each, worked in fly stitch with two threads of pink 8133. Each petal has two stitches, one inside the other. Work another fly stitch in the reverse direction in blue flower thread 2358, and a French knot in the centre in the same thread.

The sprays of white flowers are worked in twisted chain stitch with two threads, the stem in stem stitch in one thread of green 8419.

Among the larger flowers are small ones in pale blue French knots, using two threads, with yellow centres, and groups of three French knots in pink 8133 and mauve 8397.

The next large flowers are in yellow 8026 using one thread and straight stitches radiating in a circle. Small fly stitches surround the straight stitches in orange 8908 or 8129. A French knot in the centre is also worked in orange.

A group of three spider's webs in mauve 8397 are next, using two threads.

Leaves are in green 8419, stem stitch for the veins and detached chains for the leaves, using two threads.

The blue daisies are worked in flower thread in blue 2359 in detached chains with a straight stitch in mauve wool within the chain. A yellow French knot is at the centre.

A group of three orange flowers in buttonhole stitches are the final flowers in the quarter. They are worked with two threads of orange 8940 with a white French knot at the centre.

There are sprays of red French knots with green stems among the flowers; groups of French knots in orange 8129 and mauve 8397 fill in around the larger flowers.

To make up
Cut another piece of fabric 40 cm × 32 cm (16" × 12½"). Round off two corners on one 32 cm (12½") end, doing the same on the embroidered piece.

Cut a piece of fabric 90 cm × 7 cm (35½" × 2¾") for a gusset; if it has to be joined make the join halfway.

Cut pieces of the iron-on interfacing the same as for the bag and iron them to the fabric pieces.

Cut enough bias strips from the lining fabric to make 2 m (2 yds) of piping. Sew over the blind cord with a piping or zipper foot.

Baste and stitch the piping to the edges of back and front of the bag. With right sides together, join the gusset to the back and front. Trim the seams. Turn right side out and press the seams carefully.

Turn under a hem of 6 cm (5 cm finished) at the top of the front and back of the bag (2¼"–2" finished). Machine stitch, then machine stitch again 1 cm (⅜") towards the top.

Cut two strips of the bag fabric 32 cm × 7 cm (12½" × 2¾"). Sew these along the long sides to form two tubes. Trim the seam and turn right side out, press and pull over the dowels. Gather around the ends, turning in a small amount. Pull up and fasten off securely.

Screw the screw eyes into the ends of the dowels. Insert the dowels into the hems of the bag.

Make two twisted cords 70 cm (27½") long of black knitting wool, and thread them through the screw eyes on one side of the bag. Join the cords with an overhand knot 10 cm (4") from the ends. Trim the ends and fluff out the wool to make a tassel.

To make a twisted cord, take four 120 cm (47") lengths of the black wool. Tie to a sewing machine bobbin case, put it on the bobbin winder and work the machine slowly. Hold the wool fairly loosely. When the wool is tightly twisted, bring the other end to the end on the bobbin, holding the centre tightly. Let the wool go and it will twist on itself. Give it a pull down the whole length to even out the twists.

Remove from the bobbin and tie an overhand knot in the end.

Garlanded Jumper

The chunky embroidery on this jumper is embellished with beads to make a very rich garland of flowers around the neck and armhole seams.

You will need
jumper with a crew neck
DMC Tapestry Wool in:
   dark blue 7820
   blues 7797, 7283
   mauves 7243, 7242
   pinks 7153, 7155
   magenta 7157
   turquoise 7952
velvet yarn in magenta and red *OR*
   Perle Cotton No. 5 in red 321 and magenta 600
glass beads in red and mauve
sewing cotton to match beads
tapestry needles Nos 20 and 22

Garlanded Jumper

The design (see next page) is a repeat pattern 13 cm (5⅛'') long. It may need a little adjusting to fit particular jumpers. The easiest way to do this is to make the smaller flowers a little larger or smaller, or even eliminate some of them.

Baste a line 5 cm (2'') down from the welt all around the neck, and the same distance from the armhole seam towards the neck. The armhole embroidery needs to be tapered to 2.5 cm (1'') under the armhole.

This basted line acts as a guide for the embroidery. Work out the repeat pattern and mark the centres of the large flowers with a cross stitch. In the jumper illustrated the centres of the flowers are 9 cm (3½'') apart.

Start at the centre front of the neck and work the large flowers in oyster chain stitch in blue 7797, making six petals in this colour first and six in mauve 7243 in between the blue ones. Leave a circle in the centre of the flower 1.5 cm (⅝'') in diameter. This is filled with French knots in magenta 7157 with red glass beads sewn among the knots, using double thread.

Work similar flowers each side of the first one, with the colours reversed and spaced to fit the pattern. Use mauve glass beads among the knots in the centre.

Next work three oval flowers in buttonhole stitch using pink 7153. These have a bullion knot in the centre in blue 7283, and a group of three mauve glass beads between the flowers, at the centre.

Spider's webs in magenta 7157 and red velvet yarn are placed beside the group of buttonholed flowers, and a third one in magenta velvet yarn against the neck edge.

Spaces are filled with French knots in dark blue 7820, purple 7242 and blue 7283, in groups of three.

Groups of three fly stitches in half a strand of turquoise 7952 are worked at the edges of the design, with groups of three red glass beads.

Continue the pattern around the neck and repeat around the armholes.

To finish, press the embroidery lightly on the wrong side into a well padded surface.

To prevent the embroidery rubbing or wearing on the wrong side, a bias strip of fine cotton voile or silk, to match the jumper, can be sewn over the back of the embroidery. Make sure the stitching does not show on the front.

If another colour scheme is chosen, the embroidery should be a rich harmony with a small amount of a contrast.

Detail showing chunky wool embroidery and beading

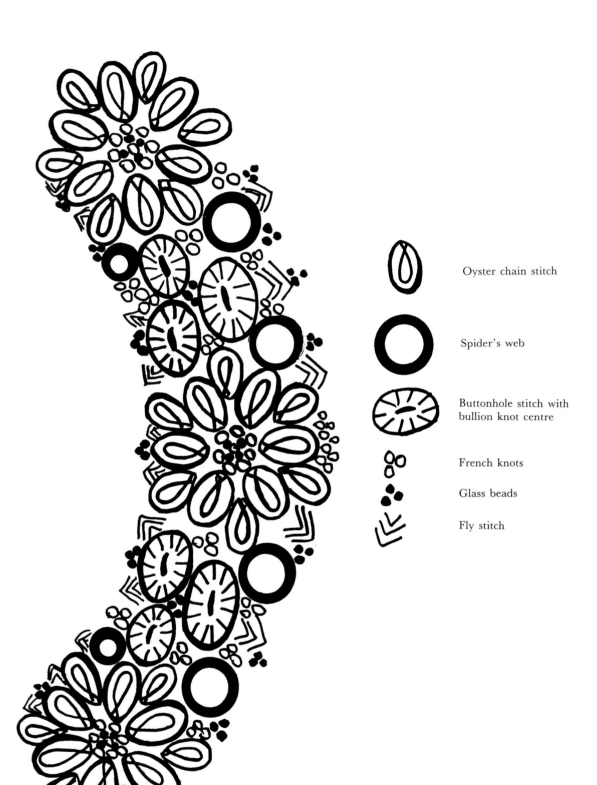

Oyster chain stitch

Spider's web

Buttonhole stitch with
bullion knot centre

French knots

Glass beads

Fly stitch